CEDARHOME
POEMS BY
BARTON SUTTER

FOREWORD BY W. D. SNODGRASS

CEDARHOME

BOA Editions
New Poets of America Series

CEDARHOME
POEMS BY
BARTON SUTTER

FOREWORD BY W. D. SNODGRASS

BOA EDITIONS / BROCKPORT, N. Y. / 1977

Grateful acknowledgment is made to the following journals in which some of these poems or earlier versions of them first appeared: *Dacotah Territory, North Country Anvil, The Small Farm, Syracuse Poems 1975, Trees, Poetry Northwest.*

Designed and Printed at the Visual Studies Workshop, Rochester, New York.

First Edition

ISBN 0-918526-03-5 - Cloth
     0-918526-04-3 - Paper

For Annette

CONTENTS

FOREWORD /W. D. SNODGRASS

SONG FOR SONG /13

DECLARATION OF DEPENDENCE /14

TALKING TO GRANDPA EASTMAN /16

LOVE POEM /17

WARMTH /18

LOVE IS WHO YOU MAKE IT WITH /19

I LOVE YOUR CRAZY BONES /20

DEATHWATCH /21

NIGHT SHIFT: THE COMPOSING ROOM /23

A CURSE AGAINST THE OWNER /24

HOMING /25

SWEDE /26

TRYING TO DREAM UP AN ANSWER /27

NIGHT LIGHT /28

NIGHT OUT /29

STALKING THE WILD MUSHROOM /30

CEDARHOME /32

WHAT THE COUNTRY MAN KNOWS BY HEART /35

DAYBREAK /37

FOREWORD

Most Americans can detect excrement miles away and will
accept no substitutes. Like his compatriots, Barton Sutter has
a sharp sense of the phoney, the plastic, the spoiled, the faecal;
he has, however, no compulsion to roll in it. If you aspire to
pay high prices for fake food, fake songs, fake saviors, fake
feelings, he is likely not your poet.

For all that, how utterly American his poems are. What is more
typical than "Night Shift"? Not merely in its pungent detail,
but in the predicament and attitudes of this crew whose work
is its despair and its salvation. One is an ex-pianist; one, an
ex-novelist; in the print shop, each keeps a pathetic pseudo-
contact with his art form. They, themselves, are "like a tropical
moth in a killing jar." Yet, their job does give them a
"justification," a proof that "These men are good for some-
thing." Work does help deprive them of self-fulfillment;
it gives them a group identity, comradery, and some modest
accomplishment to take the place of that lonely and dangerous
self-fulfillment they almost certainly hadn't the ability or
nerve for.

In "Night Out" the despair has no relief. Lenny Benson and one Diana hunt for a salvation outside work, after work -- what is more American than that? Or than the vacuity they find? "A Curse Against the Owner" stands with the best of its kind -- "The Traveller's Curse after Misdirection" or "A Glass of Beer." It, however, is not directed against any innkeeper, bar maid, or even landlord, but against "the owner" -- someone richer, farther, more corporate and abstract.

And Sutter usually writes from the viewpoint of the renter, the lessee, the immigrant. In "Swede," "Talking to Grandpa Eastman" or "Declaration of Dependence," we come back to those immigrants (or their children) whose dreams and despairs Willa Cather portrayed so tellingly. Yet there is a tone here rising above that despair. No doubt our times are less obviously hopeless; we have passed the Dust Bowl, the Great Depression. Still, we have the Great Inflation, the affluence that leaves most of us no less desperate. The poems' triumph lies most often in a tone of self-reliant skepticism and knowledge of fact, a tough, sour survivability. On the other hand, in "Cedarhome," the poet consciously adopts the sinewy, unpretty virtues of the cedar tree both for his emblem and for his coffin. Not that those virtues make the speaker sufficient to cope with America or with the world. They will destroy him, too; but he will go down with mind, wits, sensibility intact and operating.

Much of these poems' success lies in their acceptance of their own background, a refusal of the various disguises, evasions, pretensions to grandeur. Here is nothing of hierarchy, meta-physics, surrealism, the literary and spiritual forms of high church imperialism which tempt those held down by the imperial system, those envious of prestige and dominance. So these poems need not turn against those small delights which alone make life bearable for nine-tenths of the world -- house, family, friends, lover. I do not know whether Sutter will go on working in a print shop. What I could not imagine is Sutter living privately off the proceeds of affluent American imperialism, while pretending poverty so he could publicly attack that imperialism's immorality.

10

Though these poems are notable for the dry, flat tone of our common life, they surely do not lack in magic or exuberance. One could scarcely ask for more energy of imagination than we get in "Stalking the Wild Mushroom," "Love Is Who You Make It With" or "I Love Your Crazy Bones." In her least parts, his lover *does* contain the most overpowering forces of Nature; she remains a very real girl, bristling with elbows, fingerprints, toenails.

Finally, these poems have a quality which is the artistic counterpart of the virtues one can occasionally find in a good, independent auto mechanic -- one who has given up the shoddy glories of the race track and the shoddy wealth of the dealership. He has settled down with what he really cares about -- how these blamed things work -- what is important enough to live with even if (and perhaps because) it takes the place of prestige and money. The real artists and craftsmen I've known (like the few good, independent mechanics) have usually been pretty toughminded, sour types, yet basically happy, too; they were among the very few permitted by this culture to be fulfilled and free -- that is, totally enslaved to their work.

W.D. Snodgrass

SONG FOR SONG

Let me make this
Full of the moon
And right as rain,
Strong enough
To warm the guts
Of some poor soul
Like raw moonshine.

DECLARATION OF DEPENDENCE

I write to avenge my mother's death.
I dreamed of becoming a woman
For my father's sake. I have become one.
My father remarried and left me
To fill the empty place
Beside her grave like a man.
I'm doing the best I can.

I write for Scandinavians
In English. I send off my poems
Like underwater cablegrams.
Asleep, Norwegian fishermen haul up their nets
Full of foreign fish they cannot name.

My words are food
I feed the tiny octopus
Sewn up in the sack I carry
Below the belt.

I am reciting the words
To make myself a prince
Who will kiss and wake
The beauties asleep in the woman
I have always loved.

If the moon is a woman
I write for the man in the moon.
I write for wind and rain
As if they could give a damn.

I write for the wolf and loon.
I am the poem
My dreams write
For the crows who cover me in my sleep.

I have nothing to do with it.
I am the dream
Daydreamed by immigrants.
My poems are my own
Crude translations.
I know I will never come true
But this is what I have to do.

TALKING TO GRANDPA EASTMAN

What did you think, restless one?
Sex was artificial respiration?
While your wife stood by your daughter
And helped her die, you did your bit,
Chasing women as if life depended on it.
That daughter of yours was my mother.
Am I supposed to forgive you?

If it's any comfort, I haven't cried
Over her dead body, or yours, for years.
I know the sauna of sex can make a man
Come cleaner than confession, and how,
For whipping up the blood, taboos
And guilt will do more than cedar boughs.
So how am I supposed to forgive you?

Forget it. Rest in peace,
Whiskey breath, wrestling partner,
Riveter of ships and women.
You held yourself together,
Called Christ a crutch, lived
And died for your own damned sins.
I won't dig up this dirt again.

LOVE POEM

Me on my back, you your front,
We sprawl out lazylike.
The smooth of your side looks cool
As milk in a metal pail.
Tastes a little like it, too.
Now that buttersoft, secret,
Sweet saltlick between your legs.
Now I lay me down on you.

WARMTH

Sometimes want makes touch too much.
I hold my hands over your body
Like someone come in from the cold
Who takes off his clothes
And holds out his hands to the stove.

LOVE IS WHO YOU MAKE IT WITH

Find the grown up
Girl of your dirty dreams.
Ask her if she'd like to
Act out the immorality plays
You've written in your head.
She probably has her own
Rosary of obscenities. Be good
And she'll pray hot hell in your ear.
Thank her: Play priest. Make her confess
Her fantasies. Then say she's God,
Her will be done, and do it. Go down
On your knees. Call it communion.
But keep it light. If you want to,
Make something of it.
If she wants children, feel free.
But then don't call her "Mother"
Anywhere but in bed
Where you can make it clear
You know she has made you
The lucky motherfucker you are.

I LOVE YOUR CRAZY BONES

Even your odds and ends.
I love your teeth, crazy bones,
Madcap knees and elbows.
Forearm and backhand
Hair makes you animal,
Rare among things.
The small of your back could pool rain
Into water a man might drink. Perfect,
From the whirlpools your fingers print
On everything you touch
To the moons on the nails of all ten toes
Rising and setting inside your shoes
Wherever you go.

DEATHWATCH

1.

This woman is nobody's woman.
She is dead. Rosaries are said.

The mortician, a run down wind-up toy,
The Monsignor, smooth as coffin silk:
These are good men, family friends.

The father has more grief than he knows
What to do with. He takes out his wallet
As if he could give it away.

Sisters survive her.
We who love them stand by,
Guilty with good luck. Careful.
As if each of us held a brimful
Water glass in both hands.

The widower is a black widow spider,
A bomb, a radioactive pile. No one goes near.
He stands, his hands holding each other,
Head bowed in a kind of shame,
Like someone left over after all
The sides have been chosen.

2.

Warming up in their truck,
The diggers wait.
They forgot to cover the backhoe tracks.

The casket has the blue-gray look
Of lakes in hunting weather.
We sing a song. The others leave.
My lover feels the coffin
Like a forehead for fever,
Finds no warmth, and weeps.
I am no comfort.

It's hard to leave the grave
To those who do
The lonely work they do with dirt.

    3.

Friends find the family
Drawn up in a circle,
Dealing out cards and jokes.

A sister tells one on her sister.
"Laugh?" she laughs, "I like to died."
And then begins to cry.

I step outside.
The moon floats like ice
In a dark drink. Whatever
You're supposed to do with
Death is a mystery to me.

The hands on my wristwatch
Make a little phosphorescent
Checkmark in the dark.

NIGHT SHIFT: THE COMPOSING ROOM

They clock out and wait, worn out,
Too sick of words for words, a jumble
Of odd characters, shiftless night shift types:
The pianist famous for typewriter riffs,
The karate expert, the Armenian author,
The teetotaling nightclub singer,
The ex-con gone straight who still prefers to work at night,
The drunk so pie-eyed print rightside up looks upside down.

Shut-down. The fluorescent night light flutters,
A tropical moth in a killing jar. The linotypes, complicated,
Man-sized mousetraps, are all baited with manuscript.
The slugs and saws and presses are left to their own devices.
Repro proofs, displayed like choice cuts of meat, prove
These men are good for something.
The bright boil and buzz of machinery
Turned down to a glimmering hum,
The foreman puts the lid on it.

The crew crowds onto the lift, survivors on a life raft.
The author scrawls "Day shift eats it" on the wall
And gets a laugh. The elevator lets them down.
Good night. Good morning. Good night.

The Armenian rewrites the great Armenian novel in his sleep,
The blackbelt breaks gold bricks, the piano player
Turns into a player piano. The singer sweats in the spotlight
And scrabbles his lyrics, the drunk gets drunk
By something inky and bigger than he is.
The ex-con, caught in his nightmare,
Dreams he is sentenced to forty years of hard labor.
They shuffle the messy proof and try and try to justify
The same old ragged copy, the stories of their lives.

Meantime, it's morning, the dayside comes on.
They find the alphabets, letter by letter, in every case,
Bits of lead, distributed, like tools in well kept kits,
Rough-cut jewels they've inherited.

A CURSE AGAINST THE OWNER

Lord Cockroach, Old Sir Empty Belly,
Bring this bad man down.
May his woman's womb ripen
With children blessed
With testicles for ears
And breasts behind their knees.
May he have more than he bargained for.

HOMING

The river whispers the way
My grandmother used to talk to herself.
I lean against a tree and listen.
When I open my eyes, my frozen
Breath waits in the air,
Ready to break into speech.

Ahead in the path, tattered birch bark:
Pages torn from a book.
I have forgotten
The language in which the story is written.

But I know the story by heart.
I shrug my shoulders, shift
The weight on my back.
My feet read the braille of the path
I follow. I know this story. It ends
In fire, food, all the old friends.

SWEDE

1.

He's a big man with a brogue.
Americans who have never seen Sweden,
We greet his words with grins.

Never mind, old man. Tell us again
How Olsdotter, Sutter, Anderson, Olson,
Names of the dead, live on with us.

2.

When the lampreys arrived the lake trout died
And the town's fame faded.
Now the buildings are all one
Washed up driftwood gray.
The Swede is only local color,
Sitting captive in his captain's chair,
Watching the sunset, watching the waves
Leap like salmon in the red light. Look.
The waves break their backs on the rocks
And die in pools of their own making.

3.

He is troubled by his heart. He feels
Something wrong with Lake Superior.
In the white boat every night now
He hauls up his nets and picks from their holes
A few slippery eelfish, a few whitefish.

Seasick, he wakes his wife, who
All night has been riding a bike
From Stockholm down to the Baltic Sea.
She has heard all this before
But she listens again as though
His dreams were shells, shells which held
Sounds of a colder sea.

TRYING TO DREAM UP AN ANSWER

Like a compass needle
I keep coming back.
I can't explain the attraction,
Though I keep imagining this vein of ore
Turning to blood beneath a ridge
That would explain everything.

All morning, up to my neck in sunlight,
I have dozed in this clearing
Trying to dream up an answer
To why I have come so far.
As if dreams told only the truth.
As if all these miles meant something.

NIGHT LIGHT

The storm has passed. A fox barks back
In the hills. The silence is so deep
I call the blood beating my temples
A bird, drumming on a hollow log,
A bird, dancing in the dark,
Far off. I tell myself, "Now
There's nothing to be afraid of,"
And smile at that, hearing my mother's voice.
She has been dead for many years.

Dripping trees fill the stillness after I speak.
I huddle over a small fire
And watch the wet wood smoke.
The birches around me are bare;
Clean as bones, they glow in the dark.

I will sit up all night. I will listen,
Listen for the bird
Who will pass on
The rumor of sunrise.

NIGHT OUT

Ten p.m. Half lit, Lenny Benson
Roars up the highway,
Six-pack on the seat beside him.
He pounds the steering wheel, old friend,
The night has just begun.

Deer, driven out by haunch-high snow,
Crowd close to the road. Their eyes
Reflect headlights as well as anything
Put out by the highway men.

He stops at the Dew Drop Inn
For a quick one, picks up Diana.
The road is a frozen river.
Lenny fishtails all the way
To Thunder Bay and back.

Four a.m. The Dew Drop Inn's gone dark.
In the booth where she dropped, Diana
Dreams of another man.
And Lenny Benson, two parts drunk,
One part dream, one part Lenny Benson,
Slips in his chair, slips toward sleep, but fights it,
Aiming his empty beer glass like a flashlight
At the head of the dead wolf on the wall.

STALKING THE WILD MUSHROOM

Gourmet's roulette.
You need a guidebook
And lots of luck.

They are all in the same family:
Brothers to the frost
That jacks up the sidewalk,
Sisters to the terrible
Secrets of children.

They go up
Like tiny atomic bombs, something
Come near out of nothing
And going back again.
They must loom
Like water towers
To an ant, like shade trees
To a worm.

I find them
Beside an oxbow of old highway.
The freeway runs right by them,
Hissing like rain
In another world.

Those, disguised as clams,
Clinging to tree trunks
Like barnacles, are no good.
But these, tender, no bigger
Than the penises of three-year-olds,
Are good to eat. They feel
Much like the breasts of women.

I collect them. I take them home
And fry them alive. In the pan
They seem to complain
And I murmur something
Comforting,
Something like "Mushroom,
Mushroom." I can't wait.
I put one where my mouth is
And think of elves.

Don't laugh.
It's a serious business.
People have died.

CEDARHOME

1.

Make no mistake. The cedar
Is no weeping willow,
Has nothing to do
With women washing their hair.
What then? Hunchback? Gnome?
It isn't either. Whatever
Shape it assumes — pueblo ladder
Leaning into the skylight,
Upright as fire, crouched over
Like some dumb oversized
Bird that migrated into the muck
Of the early paleozoic —
Its feathery leaves are evergreen.
Cedar is a survivor.

It takes root
And stays root,
Becoming whatever it clings to.
It likes lakes and rivulets,
Swamps and sloughs, the dark beer
And winesap of things
Seeping back to ground zero.
It sucks them up, it lifts them from nothing
Up to its crown and leaves them there.
It wants wet, but lacking that,
Can pass as a cold country cactus,
A patient, camel kind of plant,
Survive on blasted granite switchbacks.
Cedar is sinewy, tougher than we are.

The way cedar trees
Smell makes me think
Of things I like to drink:
Wellwater, gin, after-the-rain jasmine tea.
They smell like star anise,
They smell like the sea.
They are none of these.
Cedar is a thing in itself.

2.

Just learning to talk, I watched
My father's father shiver cedar shakes,
Slit them to splinters
With a flick of his jackknife,
Shave off curls, auburn, blond,
To kindle kitchen stove and furnace.
My mother kept her wedding dress
In a cedar chest to stave off
Moth and rot. She trusted cedar
With special treasures.
My father taught me to know one
When I saw one.

Cedar must be my relative.
Around it, I turn primitive.
I take one for my totem.
Why not? The tree has a worthy history.
In paintings by Zen masters
They often appear, not quite there
In the mist. American Indians
Censed themselves with sage
And cedar. Swedes and Finns
Built saunas out of it
And whipped their wet bodies
Ruddy clean with greens of it.
Solomon beamed a temple
For the tribes of Israel
With the cedars of Lebanon.

3.

Can you believe it?
The Bible says: "Heaven
Lies north through the cedars."
I have doubted the word
But never the tree's
Fine facticity.

I once thought the twisted
Trunks perverted. And then one night
By firelight I saw the light:
The torque of the trunk tightens
In proportion to the persistence
With which it screws into muck and bedrock.
And the cedar's positive power
To retain and loose life after death
Proves, inversely,
The force of the process aforesaid,
Releasing, of course, the corollary:
To wit, death is only apparent,
Not nought.

How could I doubt it?
Hell, I was burning the evidence!
The deadfall I'd cut to the heart
Undid rivery ribbons of fire and smoke,
Streamers untwisting into the heavens.
What a warm, what an empirical proof!

The island I was on was adrift, a raft,
And the moon hung up
On a branch like a lantern. And then,
As if I needed a talking to,
A straggling line of geese,
A whole host of snows and blues,
Floated over, gaggling north.

4.

I didn't used to care much
What they did with me after I died.
Now I think I'd like to be planted
In a coffin knocked out of cedar planks.
What sweet seasoning that would be,
What a sloughing of flesh, what a mulch,
What peat-rich mouldering,
What lingering commingling,
What a cedarhome.

WHAT THE COUNTRY MAN KNOWS BY HEART

1.

Why he lives there he can't say.
Silence is the rule.

But he knows where to look
When his wife is lost. He knows
Where the fish that get away go
And how to bring them back.
He's learned about lures
And knows how deep the bottom is.

He has been lost and found
Where he lives moss grows everywhere.
He's made his way home
The way gulls fly through fog,
Find where water turns to stone.

In country covered with trees
He can find the heartwood
That burns best.
He can find his wife in smoke.

He knows where to look for rain
And why the wives of city men
Can not stop dreaming of water.

2.

When loons laugh he does not;
He waits for what follows,
Feeling the meaning of animal speech
Crawl in the base of his brain.

But he knows there are no words
To answer the question the owl has kept
Asking all these years.

He knows a man alone
Will begin to talk to himself
And why at last he begins to answer.

3.

He would never say any of this.
He knows how often silence speaks
Better than words; he knows
Not to try to say as much.

But then he won't say either
How often he longs to break the rule,
How unspoken words writhe in his throat
And blood beats the walls of his heart.

DAYBREAK

A goldeneye whistles across the lake
And the dream breaks. I get up;
I go outside to see what's up.

It's one of those mornings.
No matter how softly I step,
I knock lichens off their perches,
Birds and animals disappear.

I walk to the water's edge and kneel,
Drink cold handfuls of my reflection.
When I am done I am still there.

CEDARHOME has been issued in a first edition of seven hundred copies. Four hundred copies are in paper and two hundred and fifty copies are in cloth, fifty of which are numbered 1-50 and signed by Barton Sutter and W. D. Snodgrass. Fifty additional copies have been specially bound; twenty-six copies are lettered A-Z and signed by both poets; ten copies are numbered I-X, signed by both poets, and include a poem in holograph by Barton Sutter; fourteen copies are numbered i-xiv, signed by both poets, and retained for presentation purposes.

Born in Minneapolis in 1949, Barton Sutter was raised in small towns in Minnesota and Iowa. He attended Bemidji State College and received a B.A. from Southwest Minnesota State College. After working for two years as a typesetter in Boston, he was awarded the Cornelia Ward Fellowship in Creative Writing at Syracuse University where he received an M.A. in 1975. He is currently employed by a book-and-job shop in Minneapolis.

Barton Sutter has been selected by W. D. Snodgrass for BOA Editions' New Poets of America Series; CEDARHOME is his first collection of poems.